Song of a Journey-woman

Jacqueline Buswell

Song of a Journey-woman

Acknowledgements

Some poems have been published previously,
sometimes in slightly different form:
'I'm tickled pink' and 'song of the journey-woman', *4flaunt*, 2012
'the dizzy ones', *2flaunt*, 2009
'on the Bolivian Highlands', *Five Bells*, NSW Poets Union, Autumn 2008
'mutant city', *Five Bells*, NSW Poets Union, 2005/6

Some poems have also been published in the following anthologies:
'postcard to metropolis', *Our Women's Work* (Women Writers Network 2013)
'first emperor', *Read Me* (Sydney University Students Anthology, 2011)
'mutant city', *Mood Cumulus* (Central Coast Poets Inc. Anthology, 2006)
'extended family', *Off the Path* (Central Coast Poets Inc. Anthology, 2010)
'existential rag' and 'missing', *The Cows Have Been There The Whole Time*
(Bundanon Workshop Anthology, Australian Poetry Centre, 2008)
'villanelle at 64' and 'when you speak', *Voices from the Meadow*
(Wollongong Poetry Workshop Anthology, Five Islands Press, 2007)
'exile', *Hot Off The Press* (Women Writers Network, 2005)

I have been privileged to work and talk with many fine poets at the
Fairy Meadow and Bundanon Residential Poetry Workshops. I would
like to thank the tutors and fellow poets there, as well as members of
workshops run by the Women Writers Network and the Round Table at
the NSW Writers Centre. Many thanks also to the tutors of the Master
of Creative Writing at the University of Sydney.

Song of a Journey-woman
ISBN 978 1 74027 818 8
Copyright © text Jacqueline Buswell 2013
Cover design: Jacqueline Buswell and Eileen Haley,
based on a photo by Karin Hauser

First published 2013
Reprinted 2015

Ginninderra Press
PO Box 3461 Port Adelaide SA 5015
www.ginninderrapress.com.au

Contents

country	7
how we lost the peacekeepers	9
the wattle tree	11
all the world's a poem	12
abstracts	13
dawn call	15
H_2O in New South Wales	16
shipwreck	17
fire and rain	18
light moment	20
song	21
song of the journey-woman	23
northern sky	24
the first emperor	26
existential rag	28
sweet counterpoint	30
harmonies	31
the dizzy ones	32
extended family	34
glimpse of Buddhism	35
Villanelle at 64	36
missing	37
from the campsite	39
black dog incarnate	41
we share the streets	43
when you speak	45
we share the streets	47
conversation on high	48
mutant city	49

on the Bolivian highlands	50
Mexico City	51
earth and firmament	52
assumpta est Maria	53
Death at Law	55
eleventh hour	57
postcard to metropolis	59
Tijuana Freeway	60
waking in detention	62
on release from Villawood	63
possibilities	64
exile	66
madness	67
Baghdad window	69
sure stars	70
the search for peace	71
speaking about war	73
tilted jars	75
eleventh hour	78
song (reprieve)	79
cabbages	81
change the only constant	83
sequence	84
bridge night	85
footwork	86
I'm tickled pink…	87
word pulp	89
Brighton to Bondi	90

country

how we lost the peacekeepers

This story was given to us at a commemoration of the 1816 massacre near Appin, NSW.

this was tribal meeting ground
here, fighting was forbidden

once every generation the elders came
from coastal regions north and south
from the mountains and out west
and if any conflict were unresolved
they did not leave

that ceased after the killing years

the mob from up mountain would come
when the rains failed –
there was more tucker in this country

that mob was here then, they had the first
big trouble with the squatters
a man came back to his camp:
the women and children were dead
their hands cut off

he went then and killed
some white fellas

that's how the war began
killings here and there

the drought broke that very week
the soldiers marched on a governor's orders
marched in the rain at night   found the camp
killed everyone
who didn't jump the precipice

Wrapped warm in the smoke of the welcome to country
we stand in the altered landscape of Cataract Dam
on sandstone old in echoes gold in sunshine
Under the dam lies strong dark basalt

The storyteller names warriors, women, settlers, soldiers
and half-forgotten place names of an old geography

When the call is made for descendants to stand
six members of the Dharawal people come forward.

the wattle tree

The wattle tree by the machinery shed
blooms its heavy scented yellow.
The farmer takes his axe –
the harvester can't make the turn
that tree is in the way.

His wife protests, she loves its shape
the low hanging branches where
their child used to play.
The boy – she says – would hate to see
you chop down that tree.

The farmer holds his tongue. It would
indeed be good to hear that voice
reclaim. If he'd been there that day he's sure
his son would not have died.
But he'd been harvesting the wheat.

He stops these thoughts and swings
the axe, the last branch falls.

He leaves the stump, not seeing there

all the world's a poem

the sun winks behind palm fronds
white lips of wave touch the cliff
Mexico's feathered serpent flies above Thirroul

where citizens pace to and from the beach
I run to join them, ceding passway
to the Camden Soil Mix truck

trains toot and rumble
red-hot pokers rise atop the green
at night a juggler throws fire sticks by the sea

abstracts

you are at ease in this landscape
of brown grey lines and twisting bark
gnarled deformities on old trees
all dry and crackling in the heat
fallen branches force you into detours
you get lost in the abstraction
you find a sunken billabong
hear the screech and laughter of birds

on a full-moon night you watch the heavens
and shadows move around the shining bark
small creatures move in the rustling silence
you hear the plaint of the mopoke voice
a house was lost in a bushfire, you re-created
that destruction on a murky canvas

dawn light opens on a granite rock and you see
the saltbush plain stretching west below
you realise you have never seen these distances
and a kangaroo is watching you

the valley turns with swaths of orange   settles to dun
the bird song ceases and you cast about for shade
you realise you'll have to build it
you've seen the humpies, as a child you used to draw them

you pull together branches, bark and leaves
brushing away termites and spiders
you lean logs against a tree
you never were a builder but by midday
you are snoozing under your rustic canopy
inhaling eucalyptus

when you wake, you begin to paint –
that gold surround of pale blue
the iron red mountain
that mopoke night

(After an exhibition by Elizabeth Cummings, S.H. Ervin Gallery, 2012)

dawn call

day breaks in the bush
I cannot tell it new

a world alive
with raucous cries
and cheerful distant laughter

the clamour subsides
as the heat rises

H_2O in New South Wales

water restrictions came into effect
five years ago

and have not been lifted since
these restrictions mean we cannot

water our gardens at certain times
or in the old way using sprinklers which

were left for hours watering lawns
nor are we now allowed

to hose down our driveways
and we have to use buckets

when we wash our cars
they say the creek is dry

but we have good clear water
always gushing from the taps

we take long hot showers
and shave our legs carefully

under the warm flow
for every litre of urine that we pass

we might use ten of water
we swim in our private pools

massage our weary muscles
in the household spa

we count our water
by the megalitre

shipwreck

The *Adolphe* would have been a handsome ship, elegant and fancy. Built and named in France, she sailed from Antwerp in her second year to perish on Oyster Sandbar off Newcastle. Today her iron hulk rests half immersed at Stockton breakwater, poised with a certain grace, as if she were not broken and unnaturally fixed to the stone and concrete of Shipwreck Walk. She lies away from harbour-side among other ruins of ships foundered on the sandbar, separated from the port she failed to reach. Crabs play along her iron beams in the ceaseless waves and feast among the shells and seaweeds there.

fire and rain

(remembering Hanrahan)

through long afternoons
we hear the summer lullaby –
voices talking cricket after lunch
we nod off near the backward square leg
as the overs go over and over

beyond the field and the silly mid-on,
heat, thirst, dust
we drag across the plains, heading
always to the false water of the mirage,
that distant shimmering something
between us and the horizon

in the hot dry years
the crops turn brown instead of gold
sheep and cattle graze on dust
till their bones litter the land
burned, our hopes and trees

we wait
for rains will come
first drops splatter singularly, loudly
skedaddle on tin rooves and cars
bounce off the hard dry earth
clouds chase across the sky
the air is electric and uncertain

thunder frightens
dogs hide under the house
children huddle under bedclothes

now the earth smells sweet and fresh
rain falls, rivers rise
calves and horses frolic in the green
sheep grow round with wool
the farmer's step is light and proud
mothers bake and sing
buy new dresses for their daughters

the downpours do not cease
to deafen us
the river overflows
floods take tomorrow's harvest
animals seek the high ground
but waters rush and whirl
dark brown with mud and stolen life
drowned, our hopes and seeds

the plains are hidden now
as water sprites caress
and create
next summer's mirage

light moment

bare bones of trees
glitter in winter light
rain drifts across the sky

sunshine fills each drop
spreads a thousand colours
rainbows on our sleeves

the sun retracts
rain finds its gravity
it beats us now
washes away our coloured capes

song

song of the journey-woman

Short cuts across parking lots
the pacing of railway platforms on the daily commute –
this is now the path
The urban walk boasts its trees and perfumes
cats sleeping on porches
seasons passing
In summer I shade my face against the lowering sun
and lengthen my stride
In winter I pull a beanie over my ears
and it's dark when I leave work
My boots wear out on concrete
This is not the terrible exhilarating winter
on the great whale acre
nor the mountain climb for a shaman's blessing
but the footpath ever rising to meet me
The adventurer's trail today leads to
the dollar earned and the bringing home of groceries
Milestones are marked by hospital visits
and tombstones casting closer shadows
The dust of this track is made of vehicle exhaust
the steepest ascent is the town hall escalator
the greenest pasture a square of park
This is my song of the bitumen
Here too is the journey-woman tallied

northern sky

I went back to your country
saw old friends and sunrises
shared meals of familiar food
met my friends' teenage daughters
and grandchildren
camped on a Pacific Ocean beach
where turning from the water I searched,
found the great old bear, then hunting
south, argued with women of Chile and
Colombia whether that constellation was
the southern cross
or not, and we joined together to decry
our friend who refused to conjecture
our origins in the Pleiades, she said she
had no time
as I had time, I crossed
the continent and dipped
my feet in the Atlantic ocean before
heading back to the central altitudes
and on the first morning there
watched the moon set
over the sleeping-woman mountain,
then in the city centre I caressed
the deep red stone of colonial churches
with my eyes
I photographed a spiky-headed punk
near that incongruent ice rink
in the main square,

remembering how you used to like punks
but mostly I stayed in my old home town
lovely as always, noisy
as ever, busier than before,
and as you have no tomb,
I did not visit the cemetery:
your absence was everywhere.

the first emperor

though I sought immortality this life ended at fifty
I bequeath to you my terracotta warriors
the entombed craftsmen are mocking me
my story lives – two thousand years the clay stands

I bequeath to you my terracotta warriors
I was a child king – no I was never a child
my story lives – two thousand years the clay stands
I trusted myself and my horses, none other

I was a child king – no I was never a child
I rode my chariots from palace to palace
I trusted myself and my horses, none other
I built a secret mud army to protect my spirit

I rode my chariots from palace to palace
giving names to mountains and prairies
I built a secret mud army to protect my spirit
and buried the craftsmen to conceal my treasure

I gave names to mountains and prairies
few then admired the folds of my warriors' dress
I buried the craftsmen to conceal my treasure
I sought elixirs to grant me eternal youth

few then admired the folds of my warriors' dress
the detail of face, head-gear, limestone armour
I sought elixirs to grant me eternal youth
first emperor you call me but do you know my name?

exquisite detail of face, headgear, limestone armour
the entombed craftsmen are haunting me
first emperor you call me but do you know my name?
though I sought immortality this life ended at fifty

(After the exhibition Terracotta Warriors, NSW Art Gallery 2010–11)

existential rag

> *d'ou venons nous?*
> *ou allons nous?*
> *qui sommes nous?*
> Paul Gauguin

he's fixing an electrical fitting on my ceiling
and asks from the ladder
what do you believe happens after we die?

I'd like to know but I'm prepared to wait, I joke
and pass a light bulb

how did we reach such intimacy
in ten short minutes?
was it the Indian music?

is he doing undercover research on eternity
in the course of building projects?

this light bulb doesn't fit, he says
do you have another?

we've got plenty of light bulbs here
not as many as there are ideas on life and death
try this one

reincarnation? ashes to ashes? eternal return?
do you believe what they told you to believe?
do you think you'll get to heaven?

will scientists reach a firm conclusion
from double-blinded random-controlled
experimentation on the after life?

we fall silent
he takes his ladder
and climbs to paradise slowly

sweet counterpoint

closely embracing they dance in the square
one encircling black arm on a white back
one outstretched black arm marks the beat

it's Monday nine-thirty a.m.
people pass by on their march to work
their step out of time with the rumba

only two people are dancing on this square
it's of cardboard
in a niche for the homeless
downtown

I stretch out my arm to turn in the dance
the town hall clock in peripheral vision
starts to spin arms flailing loses time

it rolls down the road to the spillway
nobody stops it nobody wants it

I stretch out my hand to turn in the dance
the clock falls from the bedside table
rolls down the stairs to the wharf

it spirals counterclockwise
through ocean water
without gravity without time

my fingers were marking the beat

harmonies

violinists test their bows
clarinets and oboes blow
a bassoon sighs

down the hallway
tempos away
a man lies on the floor
beside a double bass

in silence
their corpulent curves
resonate

the dizzy ones

it's a tango
piano   piano it begins

rara she sings   rolling those r's   those vowels
you're strange, all lit up and laughing
so as not to cry
into your champagne

pena, she sings
I'm sorry to see you like this
your beautiful eyes that I used to adore
now have an edgy gleam

we'll get drunk tonight, dear friend
I don't care if they laugh and call us lightheaded
everyone has their sorrows, we have ours
we'll drink tonight

> music in crescendo the bandoneon joins in
> we dance, our skirts twirl and touch
> we don't care what they call us, we dance

again, she sings, promising, threatening,
we won't see each other again
today you're going into my past
everyone has their sorrows
we'll drink tonight

we'll take new paths
our love's been grand
but look what's left

> and in the silence it's clear
> the china's shattered

(From 'Los mareados', tango; music Juan Carlos Cobián, lyrics Enrique Cadícamo)

extended family

he left his first wife for another
the children were generally loyal
they kissed their ma and told their father what to do
the old man didn't have much to say any more

the children were generally loyal
each in their own way with hugs or scoldings
the old man didn't have much to say any more
the new wife was uncertain of her place

each in their own way with hugs or scoldings
kept strong the bonds of family and tribe
the new wife uncertain of her place
the first wife matriarch in her stronghold

keeping strong the bonds of family and tribe
grandchildren round the mother's table
the first wife a matriarch in her strong hold
the old man losing power with the years

grandchildren round the mother's table
eating his gifts of seafood from the port
the old man losing power with the years
still he tries to please the growing clan

eating his gifts of seafood from the port
they kissed their ma and told their father what to do
still he tries to please the growing clan
he left his first wife for another

(After the film *Couscous* (*La Graine et le Mulet*), France, 2007, directed by Abdellatif Kechiche)

glimpse of Buddhism

a line of orange at daybreak
monks draw near with their baskets
dawn is for giving

Buddha Buddha stupa stupa
golden Buddha golden temple
silver Naga souvenir

Villanelle at 64

it was autumn when we met again
the trees had lost their leafy green
in years the land had seen no rain

I saw that time had dealt more loss than gain
your rounded summers gone, your figure lean
it was autumn when we met again

the trees were bare and stark, in the main
a few still wore their red and orange sheen
in years the land had seen no rain

our hearts no longer shared the one domain
they trembled now and jumped the years between
it was autumn when we met again

I took your arm, we walked across the plain
we kicked at stones, at the past we didn't mean
in years the land had seen no rain

when I heard your laughter, it erased the pain
now amid the pines and firs, here at last the green
it was autumn when we met again
in years the land had seen no rain

missing

he left us in the middle of things
never explained why
took his girlfriend of course – pity –
she had good ideas on the artwork

our meetings were fun
we always ate and talked a lot
I don't know why they stopped coming
so without them we planned
and catered and decorated
and cleaned before and after

it all went very well, the guests
enjoyed themselves, and the children
put on a surprise concert
it rained, we were in the back garden
we got wet at times then dried off inside
dancing

there was plenty of food
but the beer ran out
the exhibition looked great
it was not an exhibition exactly

the aim of our reunion was to make an altar
for the day of the dead
there we placed images and objects
we'd brought from Mexico over the years

and masks we made ourselves
in plaster or papier mâché
photos of our dear departed ones
marigolds candles food and drink

no one was to know her contribution was missing
and if he had come he would have played his harp
and his Mexican guitars, and sung,
but somebody had a guitar, music was made

we missed them
there are no hard feelings
just an unexplained absence
on the altar of the living

from the campsite

the bus left us at the campsite late in the day
a gruff manager pointed to where we could pitch a tent
it turned dark as we hammered down the last pegs
we probably had some evening meal but I don't remember it
we sat outside the tent in the immense night
sensing the high unknown trees about us

later in our sleeping bags I found you trembling
where are we? why are we here?
nobody knows where we are…
all night you shivered and then me too

in the morning we saw the giant redwoods
we met the friend of the friend
who had the blessed name of Day
within a week we met her friends and found work
someone lent us a van and suddenly we had
a home on wheels and an espresso machine

we made friends with our fellow workers
more than with the friends of Day
our best mates were a Venezuelan and an Austrian
an unlikely couple, they suited us, an Australian and a Mexican

we spoke Spanish and Spanglish
and shouted with Nina Hagen: *Gott ist tot*!
the friends of Day mostly had money-making dads on the east coast
from whom they were occasionally estranged
they did not much like Mexicans Austrians or Venezuelans

we enjoyed an Indian summer all October
the thanksgiving party lasted two days
we drove the van to the ocean and to gulches
testing our skills on November's muddy roads

we heard that on our first night in the tent
some Mexicans were caught stealing the harvest
from the drying sheds nearby
two people were murdered that night

black dog incarnate

the dog lets itself be dragged across the lawn
it doesn't snarl or struggle
but the policewoman strains at every step
the dog does not want to leave
this house now full of police

a man killed his wife and children
then turned the weapon on himself
surely the dog howled and whimpered
but the man was crazed, unhearing

the children were aged nine and seven
the dog looks older. It stops now at the fence
searching for a different gate

we share the streets

when you speak

1

your accent plays in my mind
the way you shape some vowels
sees me in smiles, your intonation
deepens when you pause
the lilt of your voice
pleases me, I respond
with tripping consonants
when you elucidate
and frequently we have to ask
if what we understood was what we meant

2

my anvil hurts on hearing
the leader of the opposition
so indignantly accuse and the other
bombastic, deny
loudly do they crow
we presume to understand
a fraction of the double speak
their pitch and volume are anathema to me
cara Antonella
I would hold my parliament with you

3

we ride the train
its carriages are echo full
of Babel's tongues and accents
private murmurings
schoolboy tumult, commuters on phones
the guard in spice-warm tones
chants to us at every stop
alight   stand clear   doors closing
you do not speak
I sound the fathoms of your silence

we share the streets

we share the streets
scantily clad midriff girls
women covered head to toe

bikini tops and very short shorts
chadors veils and scarves
caps worn backwards

saris   sarongs
twinsets and pearls
tunics over trousers

strapless, backless
the minimalist dressers
show their G-strings under hipster skirts
nothing's left for idle minds
to imagine

some wear long heavy black
on even the hottest days
and reveal only parts of the face

we share the streets
whose dress is best
I cannot say

conversation on high

'We were not meant to live on cables,'
said the right shoe to the left.
'Baked in the sun, soaked in the rain
I'm electrified and dizzy.'

'I like it,' said the other.
'We're closer to the firmament
free from pavement beating
and no longer running busy.'

A strong wind blustered
and the wires sailed
the right shoe shivered
but the left one soared.

mutant city

the street where children played
and women borrowed cups of sugar
is now a long expressway
and residents
keep close to the fence
as they shuffle past
the one remaining tree

terrace houses shudder
in the scrape and shake
of excavating machines
and tremble under the swing
of high cranes

developers are ready
to swoop from tall towers
they wait perhaps
for the last pensioner

on the Bolivian highlands

we measure our water by the cup
I use a little to wash my face

and keep what falls back into the bowl
for my sister who sleeps late

sometimes we cannot cook
because we have no water

once I collected some from the stream
down by the factory

it tasted of chemicals
we tried boiling it…but still too awful

I know people who
wash in puddles when it rains

or who've used
Coca-Cola on their armpits

we have many words for our containers
not big words like reservoir

small words like jugs
buckets   bowls

not fine words like basin   bath
not words for bodies of water like

river   lake
just small words
puddle   drop

Mexico City

Worst days here, the sky is white.

On a high valley floor
ringed by mountains
dirty air hangs heavy
would weigh us down
but high altitude air is thin.

Colonial buildings
of warm red stone
and distinguished grey
are dwarfed now
by the hard glass of skyscrapers.

We understand the children here
who think the sky is brown but
worst days
the sky is white
asphalt is hot
cement is burning.

We cannot walk.
We drive three million cars.

earth and firmament

The sky flares crimson. It wakes me.
When I look again the show
has closed and solace fled
from the pillow. The quake begins
at 7.19 and lasts nearly
two minutes. Moving in circles
and waves somewhere
near nine on Richter, the tremor
shatters the spines of scores of
buildings which collapse like
broken sandwiches. Five hundred
seamstresses locked in a sweatshop
on San Antonio Abad perish together.
Mothers who try to cross
the buckling rooms to reach infants
do not get there till the quake ceases.
The second tremor comes
eighteen hours later
escalating the dust and panic
of the searching and the weeping.
Even two weeks on, people are found
alive under the rubble. And in all
those days of tears we hardly see
the sky – though many would speak
to the god they believe there,
imploring or imprecating.
Finally we notice, for it is
unusual: each day beams clear
autumn sunshine and we see why
our smog-clouded mountain-circled city
once was named the most
transparent region of the air.

assumpta est Maria

organ notes crash through
the congregational silence
and Mass begins
parishioners have brought flowers fruit and herbs
for the Virgin, it is her day
the gifts make a vibrant colony
in the centre of the chapel

three satin-brocaded priests
and six assistants hold ceremony at the altar
the ghosts of absent monks hover
over rows of empty stalls
between the celebrants
and the missal-bearing faithful
who crowd together at the back
behind a wooden grille

white-robed initiates swing incense burners
spread frankincense and myrrh
through the smoky light
the choir truly is closest to the heavens
women genuflect
their mantilla-covered heads
bowed in reverence at communion

the prayers   readings   singing
are in Latin   for the Word is sacred
only the homily is vernacular:
it has been said we have made Our Lady
into a goddess   but this is not so
and if you wish to know our thoughts
on the coming elections, Mrs Sims will be
distributing information after Mass

ora pro nobis
a rousing litany accompanies the blessing of gifts
and concludes the celebration of the Virgin
who was assumed
in caelum

Mass is followed by tea and cake
and exchanges of blessed herbs
then a sudden storm
clears the holy air of
Petersham NSW 2010

Death at Law

'The client's dead, he passed away this morning.'
I asked to sit to catch my breath and so
I heard the lawyer on the phone. 'I've never
lost a man like this, on the very day.

We'll have to wait a week or two, the family
needs some time for grieving. Cancer. The chemo –
did no good.' The lawyer on the other phone
began to read the Death and Probates Act

to see what should be done in cases where
an adversary is suddenly deceased.
'Could I sign your papers,' this lawyer said.
He signed, I rose, it was clearly time to go.

I felt regret for the man who died, doctors
and lawyers at his throat. I wished for him
a better death next time around, free
of cancer, chemo, debts and litigation.

eleventh hour

postcard to metropolis

we are the millions we must perish
we are the children born of squalor
the bastard progeny of the rich
the horsemen are coming for us
already we are homeless and without water

you exclaim at the power of nature
at the floods and earthquakes that take us
but you forced us to these hillsides
that green valley with your homes and golf course –
we lived there once

you watch images of our destruction
on the plasma screens we made
you do not cry you are too tired
we are the ones we must perish

Ah, you say (and you don't watch
survivors throw lime on our bodies)
perhaps it's better this way

Tijuana Freeway

A figure moves in the corner of my eye
unclear   unfocused   yet I know him
the swing of the hips the ranchero hat
a Mexican *campesino* heading north

cars speed past him as he walks
against all regulations
along the freeway towards THE LINE:
an ugly tin fence and a parallel
higher barrier

Border Patrol vans are parked across
the arid hillocks of the no-man´s-land
beyond THE LINE

sky darkens   the figure fades
first the hips   then the hat
he begins his turn to play
run and hide   crouch and wait

in a wood-slat hut with a leaking roof
Grandma works at the mud-brick stove
shapes the dough and cooks tortillas
hushes a child kindles the flame

the waiting mother
tends a field of corn and squash
after a while she straightens
hands resting on her lower back

she gazes north
mutters something to herself
adjusts her own ranchero hat
bends again to work
plants marigolds for November

waking in detention

dedicated to Afghani refugees detained on remote islands by the Australian government

It's the boat rocking
No – my mind.

Crowded, the boat.
Its rotting timbers creaking.
By day, vast and empty blues
by night, dark and damp

but never silent:
that stinking motor
the frightened child
adults in recrimination.

Mine is high mountain country
where clouds race their shadows
down the valley
and fire warms at end of day.

Here a square of sky
closed window
hot and tiny island
that I cannot explore

for I am imprisoned.
My body lies in stupor
but my mind sees
only shipwreck.

It's the boat rocking
No – my mind.

on release from Villawood

A man is freed today, he goes to live
by sea. Long arrest behind asylum's wire
dark with loss of land and manhood's fire –
void was he of will to hope or to forgive.
From home, bad news, missed rites of death
then silence to confirm how permanent the wreck.
Slowly into focus a visitor who made the weekly trek
rich tablecloths for tea inviting deep new breath.

He buttons his coat to better hold his heart in place
when spray and salt first smart on cried out skin,
feasts his sight-starved eyes on great blue space,
turns wordless to thank his hostess, his new kin.
And she a Jew, while he to Mecca turns his face.
Their hearts surpass divides of faith and see within.

possibilities

I went to a meeting to change the world
it's been a long time – since I tried –
it is said people get the government we deserve
I hope we never earn one like that again

so I went to a meeting to change the world
we had a quick bite to eat and set eagerly
to work   we formed small groups
and started naming the world we want

we spoke in turn and out of turn
it was easy it was happy it was smiling
we want social justice and equality
we want clear rivers and fair trade

we want no more incarceration of refugees
we want our voices to be heard
we made lists of our policy demands
and tried to fit them into categories

but they spilled out all over the place
showing no respect for borders
the demand for human rights in Burma
sat right next to land rights in Utopia

public transport and children's rights
after three hours we called a halt
washed up and cleared the table
a new world begins today

some of us will work quietly
like the mud crabs on Cooks river
some will climb the hill and holler
a new world begins today   so full of hope

why am I crying?

exile

a child of the Visigoths
one thousand years ago
planted an olive tree
in Castellon

the tree was giving fruit
before the Catholic kings
expelled the Moors and Sephardim
burned heretics at the stake

olive oil flowed green
in the presses of Castellon
when Cervantes wrote a golden age
and when Goya painted darkly

Republicans died in the olive grove
and Franco's soldiers too
yet still the local families
gathered fruit

the tree has gone
from Castellon
uprooted, sold to France

and now like Goya
old and deaf in exile
must live
far from the music of Spain

madness

Northern summer, Paris, 2000.
A truck driver's video showed us
the Concorde that never took off.
Then we saw the Kursk –
more in our mind's eye –
the submarine that never came back
from the Barents Sea.

So cold and dark
down there.

Another summer passed
we were astonished again
by the fiery, audacious smashing apart
of the proud Twin Towers.

This time CNN showed events live.
A media sensation
more immediate, more tremendous
than Hollywood, Rwanda or Kurdistan.

We play with dangerous toys
tread the mill of cruelty and indifference
rape and revenge.
We lurch from horror to worse
we burn we drown we starve
we poison. We, poison.
We fall and gasp for air,
crash and break.

Careful of the fall-out
you might get hit.
You might pick up stones
like a Palestinian child
enraged against the tanks.
You may pray for this fractured humanity
in your churches, temples, mosques,
burn your incense.

Light the candles, play the music
while you can.

Baghdad window

you stand by the window
the house is shuttered
to keep out the glare and heat
it's dark
and stuffy with our stale breath

with the impatience of youth
you open the windows
but quickly shut them again
hot here but hell outside

sun shimmers on a dozen fires
from last night's bombs
we curse the invasion
its screams of fire jet
more blood on our broken walls

we miss
sweet nights of summer
sleeping on the rooftop
old moon lop-sided on the Tigris

we sweat
the stinking perspiration of fear
stifling, bitter and gloomy
it's unbearable in here
and yet
you turn from the window

sure stars

He walks and he is sure: he knows his kin and they
are good. His arms swing loose and even, his gaze
is straight ahead. From the heartland, he joins
the US Army.

A child walks the streets of Baghdad. She is sure
that in her world only some are kind. She shares
lunch in the playground and resists
her bullying cousins.

He marches, hates the war and sickens. Throwing aside
the soldier's garb he walks one night the city he invaded.
He stops to rest in the ruins of a building, he soothes
a frightened cat.

She shows herself then and sits by him; this was her home.
Her gaze is wide, all seeing. They watch
the stars dissolve.

He is old now, he limps. His gaze is wide, uncomprehending.
Trying to make life simple again, he remembers only
those hours with the girl.

the search for peace

Riding into Merida from Portugal, I crossed an old Roman
   bridge
explored the town's ancient temples and theatres the Circus
   arena
the elegant acqueduct. A good lunch was harder to find
and as I searched I saw grafitti telling:
Peace is not a period of time it is a way of life.
I could not fault this logic, indeed my memory confirmed it
with phrases like 'the hundred years war' 'the great war'
'the mother of all wars' rather than 'the period of peace'.

I think there was a time in history with a name like that
but nothing much happened. What, people made art?
Grew new foods? Played music and enjoyed themselves?
The subversive activities of peace were ended
so it could be said that peace was not a period of time
and so people would not think that peace is a way to live.

Our chances to wander amid ancient stones
like those of the cork tree fields of Portugal are few.
Most of us will never see the dolmen and the menhir
and indeed, when we do, we don't know what to think.
Some touch the stones in silence
others take measurements and calculate
a way to the universe.

I cannot look to the distant dolmen for my source of peace
for I am caught in a world where bellicose newsreaders
drown each beautiful day with outpourings of bad news and
　sadness
and where I open my door on the morning to find boys
hurling water-filled balloons and who gleefully report,
'we're bombing the neighbours!' As far as I can see
this is a dawn raid while the village sleeps.

speaking about war

I have never known war
I dance and sing by the lake
I never cease to hear of war

the first war of my days
was called Cold
we children learned duality:
us and them

uncle Digger fought in France
in a war called Great
he lived another fifty years
didn't talk much
didn't seem to like his tucker

I knew a Jewish woman
with a number on her arm
who told me some
about the hungry camp
half a century later
she always wondered why

it was the boy next door
drafted to fight in Vietnam
not me. On return
from the scorched earth
he never wanted to hear
another gunshot

I know that war can find me
if it is to be my lot
for it found
even the meditating monks
on the high plateau

I who have never known war
alone I sing by the lake
Will I ever cease to hear of war?

tilted jars

The Plain of Jars, Phonsovan, Laos

those jars you're going to see,
they're made of stone
look how long they've lasted

half buried in earth
half full of earth
the jars resist
the wear of years and wars

trees creep into them
grow old in them
crack them open

here are the jars
remains of old burial grounds
two thousand years old

visitors keep to the path –
here is a trench line
here is a bomb crater
and there, the unexploded ordnance

with no respect for living or dead
cluster bombs rained in a secret war
and even now throw deadly metal

like abandoned pyramids or dolmens
symbols of ancient cosmic thought
the jars stand

we stand among them
puzzling about the age of stone
our long survival

and unspeakable things
like undeclared war
like a driver's hidden thoughts –

please, take your child out of the truck
I don't want him to die
in my truck

'I took him to two hospitals
and neither had any blood or oxygen
for the boy
what was I supposed to do?
drive them round all night?

just as well the parents said
let's go home then

I couldn't bear the thought
of the boy dying
a spirit passing
in my truck

as it was, it took me hours to clean –
the poor little fellow's guts
were shredded by the bombie

you know what a bombie is, don't you?
looks like a tennis ball
explodes when touched –
the place is seeded with them'

three children died that day
the eldest was collecting scrap metal
for a small business
recycling the spoils of war

those jars
look how long they've lasted

these bombies –
they could last
another iron age

eleventh hour

he believed in the mission
and thought his team
had done an almost perfect job

we were fifteen seconds late –
that was his only criticism
but he didn't think
anyone else could have
done better

Hiroshima burned
fifteen seconds
behind schedule

– **song (reprieve)**

cabbages

the earth bears and supports everything
a woman waters plants on a river bank
this is a tributary joining the Mekong
banana leaves glint in the morning sun

a woman waters plants on the river bank
all parts of your story form a picture
banana leaves glint in the morning sun
she fills each bucket from the river

all parts of your picture form a story
cabbages and salad greens in rows on terraces
she fills each bucket from the river
of course the plants are strong and healthy

cabbages and salad greens in rows on terraces
half a dozen wooden steps then the earthen rise
of course the plants are strong and healthy
what makes your flower precious is the time

half a dozen wooden steps then the earthen rise
every day this simple task repeated
what makes your flower precious is the time
the time you've given it, watched it grow

every day this simple task repeated
throw the water down along each terrace
the time you've given it, watched it grow
the river will carry it all away

throw the water down along each terrace
here a tributary joins the Mekong
the river will carry it all away
the earth bears and supports everything

change the only constant

I dawdle in the car park outside Palliative Care,
a kookaburra, like me, regards the world,
and the bird and I, each other

the nurse imparts the news
in solemn tone, with grave demeanour:
my friend had passed away the day before.

We exchange a few words
   …she is resting now
   …it is a release
promptly I decide to leave
and hear as I depart –
gone from the voice
the weight of all her training –
OK sorry

as if she'd told me
the lift was out of order
and I would have to take the stairs.

From the tree of course the bird
had flown. And this was for me, as for Borges
after the death of one, his Beatriz

the first of infinite change
in the incessant universe
now moving away now different from
her life.

sequence

through the rainbow
a prophet
trousers rolled

musician
at keyboard
confounds black and white

by the sundial a poet
wearing a beret
spins crystal glass

words on granite
I sleep again

bridge night

the poets meet
they make a bridge of paper

and debate whether
to cross the viaduct

or set their words ablaze
as bridges burn

footwork

spade in hand, sweat moistening the earth
you stand in the field of corn
you with your peasant feet

your staff and bag, your cross or crescent
miles to go and mountains to climb
you walk in your pilgrim sandals

your tutu turning and your sinews straining
in one with music you spin
on the cushioned tips of your dancing shoes

your shorts and top and prancing legs
your vitamins and supplements
you in the brand-name runners

you turn our heads when you wear that dress
your toenails neatly painted
you in your red high heels

you with your cities of history
your tasty fruit, your long boot
eternally nudging Sicily

I'm tickled pink…

because the birds are singing and so am I
because the weather's cooler, and the pine trees smell
  exquisite after rain

because the boss was generous, the clients content, the
  contractors
pulling their weight, the colleagues cheerful

because the meal was good, the water cool, the conversation
  stimulating
because you talk as if you cared, you tell me things I did not
  know
because you are here with me because you exist

because I dreamed that I could live forever

but none of this is true, I am not dancing with the tickled
  pink,

because you tell me nothing, because you are not here

because the food barely passed as a nutritional requirement
the water was tepid, the conversation bland

because there has been no rain and the oak tree is covered in
  dust
because no singing can be heard in this din of yapping dogs
  and sirens

because the colleagues were glum, the contractors remiss,
the clients complaining and the boss, cranky

because the weather was suddenly cold, and I caught a chill

because I dreamed I nearly topped myself

don't even think of tickling me, there is no colour, there is no funny bone
and the mind is fragile like the great-aunt's femur.

word pulp

words like chaff, flying
words, junk to be sorted
words like a tree, growing

words on paper
a printing revolution
consumes the forest

unwanted words
shredded scraps
mulch on the garden bed

Brighton to Bondi

the concert in her own words

sirens   your divine sounds
your dreamless grief

plenteousness
builded as a city
a sapphire-coloured throne
a little wonky shack

if splendour dazzles in vain
marvel and know not

only this I want
the perfect diapason

peace in Jerusalem
and at the captain's table
only this I want
peace in Jerusalem

Sydney was dreaming
Sydney was

a cold shore
a bureaucratic harbour

England green and pleasant
mixed power employs

raining at the fountains
and at the captain's table

his ghost may be heard
you can't lose it

(Festival Chorus, Sydney Philharmonia Choirs, 2011)

www.ingramcontent.com/pod-product-compliance
Lightning Source LLC
Chambersburg PA
CBHW062141100526
44589CB00014B/1644